52 WAYS

to fund your home business

Even if

You are broke, your credit sucks
And all your friends hate you

By

Nike Roach

InteliPress Publishing

Fifty two ways to fund your home business, even if ....

Copyright © April 2014 by Nike Roach

Dedication

I would like to firstly thank my mother *Yeyefini Efunbolade* and my grandmother *Ruby Allen.* Your inspiration and perseverance in the face of adversity has always been an inspiration.

I want to thank my Aunt and Uncle; *Claudette* and *Clinton Pough* for always having a kind word to share and loaning me the money to fund my first company.

I want to also thank my mother-in-Law *Pansy Ferguson* because without her I would not have found the most amazing wife.

I would like to thank our three Boys, *Eniola, Abiola* and *Ifayori.* Your energy and vitality is infectious.

I would like to thank my friend, wife, business partner and constant encourager *Nikki*. You are the most amazing person I know.

I'd like to thank my success coach and mentor *Dani Johnson* for consistently speaking life into me.

Finally I must thank the Creator of all things for allowing me another day to make a contribution.

About Nike Roach; - the Author

Sir Richard Branson, one of the richest men on planet earth has reasoned that most of his literary inspiration is drawn from books written by people whose roots are embedded in the Caribbean, and the academic annals of Africa.

In other words, many of his business ideas and inspirations were drawn from those Caribbean and Africa rooted authors whose start-up business advises were always unpolished but frank and effective.

So when you take the Caribbean and African rooted ancestry of emerging author and successful Home Business Adviser, Nike Roach into account, you can be certain that his advises and tips in the pages of this book offers nothing less than the same degree of respectable advise that Sir Branson was referring to.

Notable for starting a successful home based business from the age of fourteen via a family loan, Nike Roach has since evolved into one of the most inspirational advisers and counselors for home based business owners

So respected are his advises that he was featured on the cover of the Home Business Advertiser magazine in 2013 as one of the top producers in his travel company.

He has since been widely considered by many as a successful entrepreneur in his own right; - since he has demonstrated unparallel successes as a health and wellness business owner, online marketer, teacher, and a business coach.

But after facing repeated requests for documented advise packets, and feeling the need to start putting his advises in a concise and self-help way, Nike Roach decided to put together this book, which holds 52 of his most successfully tested advises for emerging home based business owners, who may be struggling for funding.

It is now hoped that you will utilize this book to your benefit, and that the home based business advising skills of the author Nike Roach, may unequivocally inspire you on your way to secure business funding.

Why this book was written

Have you ever had a creeping thought in your head that you were meant for another life? -- A feeling that the job you are in was not what you really wanted to do but because the life you had chosen, you had very few options?

Well many people have that sinking feeling and start looking at home business as an option. It has the maximum business potential with minimal risk since relative to other categories of businesses, the cost to get started is extremely low.

For example, to get started in a McDonald franchise it could cost you millions just to get the licenses alone; and that does not even include the bun and fries. --- But even if you decide to take up a smaller venture that costs 0.001 percent less than a McDonald's franchise -- what do you do if you are having challenges in your life such as credit card bills, messy divorce, your spouse passes away, you lose your job, your health has changed for the worse, your family hates you, your credit sucks or you are fired?

How do you get back on your feet?

This book was written to answer that very question, and to help out those that really want to have a stable home business but may not have any clues where to find the funding, and more important how to get it so that they can get started.

This book will show you how to fund & upgrade your business so that you can get started at the top level; - because that is where the greatest potential for real rewards are.

This is an action book that has been broken up into 52 parts to correspond with the number of weeks in a year.

No matter what the season or your location, chances are you will find something to use in this book that will help you or a team member to get started.
Some of the funding sources are controversial and may even challenge your sensibility.

This book is like a buffet, you take what you can use and those ideas that don't reflect your core values, just leave it on the table for another.

At the end of the day all you are looking for is a few ideas that will help you get started so that you can make as much money as you may want, know the strategies and formula for success, create meaningful long term relationships, and have a blast doing it.

Nike Roach
Author

Table of Contents

Introduction: - What is a home based business?

 Some of the most successful home based business stories probably rest on the story of Steve Jobs, who started Apple Inc. from his garage, to Jeff Bezos who founded Amazon in his home in Bellevue, Washington, and up to Mark Zuckerberg and others who started Facebook in their college dorms.

And of course there are thousands of others self-made millionaires whose successful business stories started on a computer and a desk in a small corner of their home, or a small oven in their kitchenette.

But with the evolving trend of rapid home based business establishments and the constant overnight successes of these business, we are all sometimes caught up in asking a seemingly stupendous question. And that is; - What really is a home based business?

While the answer to the question itself seems logical, many business analysts would often erroneously or deliberately tie a home based business to the same category of a small family business, which often creates some confusion in the

1

minds of the average answer seeker.

Therefore, depending on who you ask, a home base business can sometimes have some varying, but closely interconnected definitions.

Sometimes its definitions are quite simple and easy to accept, while in other instances, it can be too complex for the average home based business owner to accept.

For some people, a home based business is simply a business launch pad that is used to nurture an operation through its embryonic stage, *(just as Steve Jobs, and several other successful entrepreneurs had done)*, in preparation for its future expansion into something larger.

However, the generally acceptable definition states that; - A home business is any small scale or medium scale lawful business operation that is principally conducted from the business owner's home, or from an office annexed to the business owner's home.

It is usually staffed by the owner only, who would serve as its marketing, accounting, and service agent, or may be supported by a small number of staffs who may basically encompass a spouse, children and or other family members.

Nonetheless, the key element of a home-based business is that it typically functions from the home of the business owner regardless of its operational scale.

And because it does not requires too much of investments on facilities, transportation and other large scale operational requirements, a home business is usually easy to set up and operate, depending on the nature of the business being referred to.

This ease of establishment has allowed millions of small home base businesses to spring up here and there every year.

But while it may seem easy to get started, a lot of folks tends to treat their home based business entity like a wrapped up candy, while forgetting that it can be foreclosed in the same simple way that it had started; unless you can ensure that certain necessities are in place for its operation, stability and growth.

Getting into a home base business *(The necessities)*

Starting a home based business has its varying steps, needs and requirements depending on what you envision to do.

But from a basic standpoint, all home businesses has certain basic requirements, which generally centers around its legality, its plan, and financing to get it off the ground.

While community zoning regulations and other primary factors can affect the smooth setting up of certain categories of home based businesses, most others are not bothered by anything more than getting the business registered, and a visit to the local tax office.

In essence, the paperwork requirements for most simplified home based businesses are usually a non-challenging issue as they are generally easy to acquire, and is even non compulsory in some cases.

That aside and has indicated earlier, you would also need a well thought out business plan, and a realistic first year budget, since it would have been unsound for you to launch a home based business without considering either factors.

However, while you may be able to acquire your paperwork, a business plan, and your budgetary estimates, you would most likely not have the required funding to get the business going as planned.

According to Forbes Magazine, almost 60% of individuals going into a home based business, usually do not have any money, hence their reason to go into a home based business in the first place.
Outside of that, just around 85% of home based start-ups do not have enough funds to effectively launch their operation according to plans, or even to operate it in a manner that will make it viable.

Using that as my guide, my wild guess would be that you are probably fitting yourself into one of those categories of new comers, who may not have the required funds to get your home base business idea on the road.

And if that is the case, I may also assume that you may probably be plunging your thoughts in despair about where and how you may be able to source the budgeted funds for your home business.

Well, at this juncture, I would sincerely like to urge you not to be despaired or be daunted by your prospects; - Because in the subsequent pages of this book, I will show you 52 simple ways in which you can raise thousands of dollars to fund your home based business initiative.

Funding your home based business
- 52 ways to get the money you need

As I had told you a few seconds earlier; there are indeed many simplified ways in which you can earn a honest dollar to properly fund your home based business operation.

And as I had promised you, here are 52 simple ways to get the money flowing in, with almost minimal effort.

For a start, one of the simplest avenues for obtaining funds for your home-based business is to locate the money that you already have.

By that, I meant you either forgot about the $2000 you had tucked under your mattress three years ago, or it's time to have a yard sale.

A Yard Sale

 My first suggestion here may seem unimpressive to some. But if you ask the financial historians at Forbes, they would remind you that the pioneers at HP, Mc Donalds, and a host of other large corporations, had to raise money by a few well

7

organized yard sales in order to fund and make their respective business ideas blossom into the giants they are today.

So if, you are having second thoughts, I would advise that you pull yourself back together and let us focus on how to raise some booming finance to fund your business,m starting with a yard sale.

As most of us would know; a yard sale is an ideal way to spend a weekend because it will not only raise money for your business but it's an opportunity to de-clutter your living space at the same time.

An average yard sale, by some estimates, can net anywhere from $1000 to $2500 in two days depending on several factors, which we'll discuss here.

Since it is not a bad way to spend a weekend, it might be a good idea to seek out some tips that can make the weekend rewarding for you and your business funding prospects.

But if my advise is good enough for you, here are a few tips for holding a successful yard sale and making as much money as possible from your efforts.

#1: Evaluate the condition of the items you plan to sell – If you don't care about the condition or quality of what you are selling, then rest assure that a bundle of unsightly and unwanted items would turn off your potential buyers who may prefer to be at a real yard sale than at a junk yard.

As such, try to make a thorough inventory of the items, and try to make a honest determination as to whether the items that you have are really fitting for a garage sale, or whether some should be thrown away as garbage, or be made into a distant junk heap for those things that you do not care to sell.

Buyers would most likely to stop and participate at a yard sale that is filled with items that are in good condition, rather than having to peruse a grouping of items that are not appealing.

So to avoid a humiliating experience for yourself and your potential customers, carefully seek out the items that are worth selling, and put away those that can kill the event.

#2: Identify hot listed and wanted items for adverts – In preparation for an online listing, local newspaper classified or any sort of advertising, you should identify items that are sure hot sellers to mention prominently in your advertising space.

Placing hot sellers at the top of adverts usually pull the attention of a higher volume of readers and prospective buyers.

For example if you have an expensive range of silver cutlery and fine China that is always in demand or an in demand range of electrical gadgets, make a note of that to include in your adverts so as to attract a wider cross section and larger number of potential buyers.

#3: Advertise well – Use free resources, such as Craigslist, Facebook feeds, Facebook invitations or events, Twitter friends alerts, and social network status message posters, to advertise in advance of your sale. Posting photos of the items you'll have for sale is also a plus!

#4: Place large items in front – On the day of the sale, you should place larger items in an area that is more widely visible to traffic and pedestrians.
This will attract drive-by traffic and encourage them to stop, park and come to your sale since you would have already enticed drivers with the large attractive items that was placed strategically at eye level from the street.

#5: Have a "free!" pile – By giving away items in a "free!" pile, you can entice customers to your sale and, hopefully, they'll take home some "not free" stuff, too!

#6: Join forces – Combine your sale with the items from neighbors so that you have a larger venue to advertise. Serious garage sale shoppers are attracted to larger sales marketed as 'multiple family' sales.

#7: Price to Sell – Price your items low enough to sell. If you have some valuable pieces that you don't want to price low, sell them elsewhere (e.g., eBay, or similar). Shoppers go to garage sales for a bargain, not to over-spend on someone else's used stuff.

#8: Clean Up – Take the extra time to clean up your items. Dusty and grungy items are hard to sell.

Pick a nice weather weekend and maybe even set up a self-serve cooler of $0.50 sodas for people to buy.

Be friendly, have some fun, and don't be shy about letting customers know you're fundraising at your yard sale to raise capital for your new home-based business.

You might be surprised by the business connections you'll make in your very own neighborhood.

#9: Think about accessibility and customer parking - You should temporarily remove your cars from the driveway, and cater for customers who may have to back in your driveway to shop and load their purchases.

Parking challenges can turn shoppers away or even limit their stay at your garage sale. Therefore, you should create two or three safe parking zones for maybe seven or eight vehicles at the same time (depending on the size of your yard sale)

You can make sure that there are adequate parking options for customers which can include seeking your neighbors permission to use the space in front of there house, where you can place makeshift stickers or signs to tell customers that they can park there if they are visiting your yard sale.

#10: Do not be a meanie: Try to be open about bargaining with your customers. You do not want to be rude with them or too reluctant about price flexibility.

Therefore, if a customer eagerly asks you to take off another ten dollars from a ninety dollars price tag, quickly weight whether it is worth refusing to sell it for less or whether it would benefit you more to keep it.

Customers goes to a yard sale with the expectations of getting extremely low bargains. Therefore, you must try as much as you can to reach out to them, as per their expectations.

A Creative Yard Sale

On the other hand, while a yard sale may be a good start, not everyone can take advantage of this method.

This is mostly because you may not have anything to sell or do not have anything of much value in your home to warrant a yard sale.

If, you are confronted by this reality, then you can still resort to what is called a creative yard sale.

A creative yard sale is just a variation of an actual yard sale, except that the items being sold are usually donated by a single or multiple sources to the person who is actually conducting the sale mostly for their benefit or for some other cause.

To effectively launch a creative yard sale for your own funding needs, you can, among other things; -

A. Write short note to 40-60 of your neighbors telling them that you are trying to seek their assistance in helping you to start your own home based business. And in your quest to raise some funds you are inclined to help them get rid of their old or unwanted stuff, which you plan to sell via a yard sale to raise some funds.

In the enclosed letter, you should send a self addressed stamp envelope so that the person can send the note back to you noting the time they want you to pick up the items from their house.

B. explain that 100% of the money will go towards you starting your own home business.

C. Reiterate that you would have asked to borrow the money but you're also looking to be creative in your funding objectives.

You can also express that you were technically looking for an investor.
But rather than just borrowing it from them, you now decided to ask your good neighbors if they have any extra stuff that they were planning to give away anyway---but which you can sell to help raise the funds that you will need to fund your business.

D. Try to acquire the last set of items at least two weeks be-
-fore the yard sale, so that you can utilize the same ten
steps that we had discussed earlier for a standard garage
sale.

After all, you would still have to reexamine the items, clean
them, tag them, advertise them, and follow the same yard
sale steps as if all of the items were brought out from your
belongings.

Blow Leaves

 One of the most amazing stories you can read on Yahoo finance, is the rags to riches episode of former leaf blower and landscaper Dave Lindahl.

Dave was a 29 year old man who was broke while living in a small apartment near Boston, and could have barely fed himself.

After being cornered with nothing much to do, he started a home based business which handled leave blowing and landscaping for a growing list of customers.

When Dave had made enough from his leaf blowing and landscaping tasks, he ventured into buying foreclosed homes, renovating them, and then reselling.

After twelve years of progress, his fortune is now worth around $143 million, and is spread across eight states.

Dave's experience has shown the level of financial gains a person can make towards the funding of their home based business, by simply embracing some leaf blowing and landscaping as a fund generation source.

In reality, leaf blowing is one of the more preferred and convenient methods that people uses to clear their yard of dropped leaves, and other unwanted tree elements.

However, since most people are not too keen on burning up their time with this task, they would usually engage the services of yard maintenance and landscaping operatives to take care of this task along with the required mulching, bagging, and efficient removal of the leaves.

But interestingly, this is a task that requires no other skills but your common sense and the ability to efficiently use the leaf blower equipment, which is nothing more than a reverse mechanical element of the vacuum cleaner.

So while most folks may be busy with other tasks or some relaxation preferences on Sundays, you can ask your neighbor to loan you his leave blower, and offer a leaf blowing service to other members of your community or neighboring communities, which can bring you as much as $1,000 on a weekend.

While the size of the yard, the number of trees, density of the leaves to be blown, and other factors can affect pricing, you can still rake in somewhere between $40 to $320 per yard, depending on the neighborhood and the financial standing of the hirer.

And even though some folks may not immediately see the need for a leaf blowing service, it may be smart for you to let them know that you are trying to raise funds for a business venture; - which may most likely coerced them into giving you the task to do, simply because they found just cause in helping you to achieve your goals.

Shovel Snow and Salt

 If you know Ingvar Kamprad, you will know that he is now one of the most powerful business magnates in Sweden, and is also one of the richest men in the world, with a fortune of over 40 billion dollars.

You will also know that his humble beginnings goes back to a home based business that sold matches to neighbors, which he financed by shoveling snow for folks in the neighborhood, and periodically selling them other items such as fish and Christmas decorations.

So if Ingvar Kamprad could have propel himself into one of the most wealthiest men in the world by selling matches, and shoveling snow among other things, then why can't you?

This billionaire's story is simply saying that even shoveling a little bit of snow for a few dollars can make a difference, even if the task appears to be too frivolous and pride cladded.

Therefore, when the snow starts falling, and the many driveways in your neighborhood starts snow clogging, then its time for you to let the dollars start rolling.

Unlike the prolonged winter conditions of Sweden where Kamprad had shoveled his success from the snow, the weather pattern in the US will demand that this job be seasonal in nature.

However, we know that this revenue earner can still easily contribute somewhere between $500 to $1,200 per week, towards your home based business.

So with a few weeks of snow, I am sure that your savings will soon start to get over the top.

To get started, simply, share some flyers and spread the news in your neighborhood, which can also take the form of Facebook and other free social mediums.

While alerting folks about your service, do remember to let them know why you are doing it, while reiterating that you will be happy for their support of your quest.

You might be surprised to see the volume of call-ups and hires you will get at various periods of the day from desperate customers to handle their snow shoveling and salt needs during or after a major snowfall.

The good thing about this is that you do not necessarily need any major equipment or expensive tools to undertake this task.

All you may need is the determination like Ingvar Kamprad, a willingness to stick to the task, and a good shovel which has a wide bottom and a long handle that may allow you to work with minimal bending and with less effort.

In extreme cases, you may want to consider a snow blower; if one can be loaned to you for a commission. If not you can hire an additional co-worker if the task will inundate you.

To make the shoveling less tiring, Kamprad who did this as part of his home based business funding routine, suggested that you should always coat the shovel blade with vegetable oil or a thin coating of petroleum jelly at home if needs be, while putting your health, safety and well-being first before accepting any snow shoveling task.

Detail Car

 Some of us would scuff at detailing cars or washing other folks cars because it somehow might not fit in with our misguided ego.

But if you consider that just over a decade ago, daytime Emmy-award winning talk show host Ellen DeGeneres was busy detailing cars to earn some cash, on her way to fulfill her dreams on television, then you would figure that you seriously have to look at this differently.

In an interview with Larry King back in 2004, DeGeneres expressed her pride in what she did and was adamant that no one should be embarrassed about taking on a car detailing gig, once it is putting an honest dollar in their pocket to fulfill whatever lawful purpose that person may need the money for.

And if you ask many other celebrities such as Detroit's own rock and roll artist Bob Ritchie, a.k.a. Kid Rock, Kevin Federline (who had worked at Red Carpet Car Wash in Fresno, CA), and Film Director John Singleton, they would all tell you that their first job started at a car detailing center.

After all, it is never a bad job to offer people a service that most of us hardly realizes that they need.

This is based upon the fact that most people drives their car everyday with an interior and exterior appearance that they wish to appear cleaner, but hardly finds the time or willingness to detail it.

Hence, in essence, they are always subconsciously in a state of needing it detailed but unable to do it themselves.

And even though others may be conscious of the fact that they also need their car to be detailed, they often do not have the time to take it to a wash bay or detailing center to have this done.

As such, it is always an attractive task to have someone coming right in their driveway during their relaxation period to have the car detailed.

Now, this is where you can earn some quick cash, if you dispatch some flyers, post some Facebook feeds or get the local newspaper to do a little feature for you, which may freely give you some exposure along with your contact information.

Getting this task can earn you a minimum of about $100 per gig, plus some easy clients, especially if you can explain your reasons for taking on the extra cash earning task.

If you have any doubts about this, go a little further and ask singer-songwriter, record producer, author and actor; Steve Earle, who had also sorted out his career financing needs by working at a car wash in Houston, Texas.

Micro Loan From 100 People

 Brett Kelly, an Android applications enthusiast from Southern California saw some documentation need for the popular business App; Evernote.

Sensing that it needs a guide system, he borrowed a hundred dollar each from ten friends just over a year ago, and bought the time of some additional information researchers to help in his quest to develop the most comprehensive tutorial for the Evernote App.

Originally expecting to make nothing more than two or three thousand dollars , he nonetheless made more than $100,000 in less than a year, from global sales of the App which was funded by nothing more than a series of small loans from close friends and associates, making over 1000% profit from his initial investment.

His business idea was easily funded because he made his move on the theory that It is harder to get someone to loan you a $1,000 but is rather easier for one thousand people to loan you a dollar.

After all, a single dollar may not be anything significant to them other than amusement.

Taking that into account, you can raise funds by listing as much trusted high school friends, relatives and associates as possible, and ask them to lend you maybe a ten or twenty dollars each, in support of your home business initiative.

To them, it may seem like a relatively small amount. But on the other hand, fifty persons loaning you twenty dollars each would easily amount to $1,000.

Again, this should be an easy task if you thoroughly explain to people what you are planning to do with the money, and go the distance to justify that it is worth their while giving you a fraction of your home based business needs.

You can do this via a letter to each person or at an arranged meeting, depending on the targeted individuals, your relation to them, and the circumstances that may have warranted a meeting between you and them.

Interestingly, once you have a few people that says yes to helping you with your project, indicate this to the next person who you are approaching to helped you out. Most people would consider things less risky if others have already engaged in the funding.

Credits Cards/ Debit Cards

 Well known British businessman Ken Wills started his now successful business empire with nothing more than a series of credit cards financing, and worked his way up to a business network with a turnover of over £20 million.

Ken's first start dependency on funding from credit cards had helped him to push a small home based business into a multinational conglomerate that encompass a jet engine maintenance company, a helicopter firm, a jewellery business, a fire prevention company, a radio station, and a restaurant.

Ken's theory is that once you do not have any bad credit, then one of the easiest ways to access funding for your home based business is to apply for a credit card with a large credit limit.

Acquiring this is usually a simple and straightforward process, which generally entails signing-up with your local bank (where you might already have an account) for a Credit Card.

Using short term funding from credit cards is usually the best option because it gives you 30 days to recoup your investment and you will immediately be able to conduct your business.

As a word of advice, you would want to make a simple credit card application, and remember to get the ones with high point to dollar ratios, since more points would mean that you can double dip some capital.

If you are uncertain about where to get a head start on this, there are some choices of credit card companies that you can consider for review online, but namely those listed at;

www.mbna.com, http://creditcards2u.com/

and at;

http://www.100best-credit-cards.com/

Home Equity Line

 With a Home equity line of credit, you should have no trouble in raising a few thousand dollars more to effectively finance your home based business.

If we should take the experiences of San Antonio, Texas millionaire Bert Butler "Tito" Beveridge II, into account, then we can get an insight into how a home equity line can positively transform the anticipated fortunes of an emerging home based business operator.

Starting from his family kitchen, Tito took cash against his home from the bank, and plugged it into a home based brewery business.

And after two years, his brewery business began to expand into what is now one of the largest Vodka brewery in the United States.

As is evident, Tito could not had been successful in his home based business pursuits without proper funding.

Knowing this, he did not hesitate to consider acquiring a

home equity line, which has proven to be a most wise decision, that had made his home based business into a multinational corporation.

The good thing about a home equity line is that it is fairly easy to acquire if you have equity in your home.

Under this arrangement, a low interest option can also be added to an existing loan if the house is not yet been paid off.

But regardless of whatever direction you take as it relates to a home equity line, you may not be far from getting the same positive results as Tito, who has transformed the investment of his equity loan into national brewing empire.

Should you require further guidance on how to acquire a home equity loan, you can check with one of the better known advisory sources for this type of financing, and which can be accessed online at:

www.lendingtree.com/HomeEquity

Borrow From Your Retirement Fund

 While most of us might be reluctant to borrow from our retirement fund, doing that is not so bad if you are going to borrow to aid in the financing of your emerging home business.

Most people mistakenly thinks that a retirement fund is just an account intended to serve any good purpose until they are age 65.

But like a bank account, you can use your retirement account to access many other banking related services, including acquiring a loan or cash advance to fund your home based business operation.

A much better known example of success from such an initiative can be taken from the CNN featured Tim Grittani, who invested a mere $1,500 from his retirement fund savings, to fund a home based stock trading business, and became a millionaire in just over two years.

While everyone's fortune may vary, Tim has taught us that effective management of a loan from your retirement account, to fund your home business can certainly be a wise choice.

To access a loan from your retirement fund, you will usually have to sit down and present some solid reasons to your retirement fund manager, as to why you need the loan. Some 401(k) plans would permit borrowing for any reason. However most would permit loans only for certain specified reasons or purposes.

While your retirement fund manager may see some wisdom in taking out a loan to pay off high interest credit card debts, he may not see any logical reason for you to borrow against your retirement fund to pay for a high priced vacation to Tahiti or for an expensive cruise trip to the Caribbean.

Even mentioning plans to start up a home based business can be risky reason if your fund manager does not believe that such an investment is viable.

As such, you should put forward a solid reason to your fund manager that would be sure to encourage him or her to grant you a loan against your retirement fund.

You can then chip some money from the loan to finance your home based business.

College Loan

 DreamWorks billionaire owner David Geffen swapped his college education fund for venturing into a home based animation business which subsequently evolved into the worlds biggest earning animation production company.

The same can be said for many other initially home based business owners, who had bitten into their college funding to simply finance their business goals.

Even though this is a negative avenue for some, by their thoughts of course; - you with a better frame of mind and optimism can similarly chip small amounts of funds off of your college loan to help finance your home business.

The simple principle with regard to this is that you must train yourself to repay once your home business starts to generate a stable income.

However, at the same time, you may want to note that; most college loans are easy to obtain if you are in school, while some states dictates that the loan can only be used for school related expenses such as a computer; in which case you can always purchase (maybe two or three units) and sell two to another person to acquire the funds.

The only disadvantages about college loans is that you cannot be relieved of it via any form of filing for bankruptcy.

Bank Loan

As a general rule, the average home based business operative will initially resort to a local bank to fund the plans of his start-up entity.

A bank loan can technically resolve your funding needs for your home business in its entirety, especially if your bank have confidence in whatever prospects you have laid out to them.

Wendy Foster, a single mom and Avon products rep from Canton, Georgia, received admiration from the Business Insider magazine, after revealing how she took a small bank loan to embrace her product marketing and sales venture.

In a 2010 interview, Wendy had approached her local bankers to fund her start-up home based business, which had basically entail the retail sale of Avon products to members of her community.

While the initial loan was a mere $8,000, Wendy took that amount and double her investments, while repeatedly taking larger loans, as she kept repaying previous loans within a short space of time.

And after more than three years of reworking her bank loans, Ms. Foster is now more than two million dollars richer, and the owner of one of the largest home and beauty care distribution networks in Georgia.

The obviously happy mother of two attributed her millionaire success to her $8,000 bank loan, a good business plan, and her financial discipline as an emerging home business owner back then.

She is sure that a properly managed bank loan, no matter how small it is, can make a big difference in the successful evolution of a home based business.

And even though some banks today may be reluctant to fund certain categories of home based business initiatives, you can still make the application for other purposes and divert some of the funds to your business ideas.

In other words, a bank loan application does not necessarily have to be directly attributed to your home based business project, if it will not win the confidence of your bank.

As such, and as unethical as it may seem; it may be better to source the loan for vacation or some other easily approving purpose, and filter a needed portion of it to your home base business funding needs.

Again, you may still need to adopt some principles, and ensure that you repay the loan, as soon as your business starts to generate some income, and at least within the time frame and conditions stipulated by your bank.

While a bank loan may be a good option, it can be a little tedious to achieve, since it may require that you have a good credit rating, as they generally would not loan you less than $10,000.

And if you have the patience, it can also take several weeks to be approved.

On the other hand, most credit unions with which you are associated with can also serve this purpose but may generally have stricter rules.

When you require a small loan, the average typical bank and several other commercial lending sources may often turn down a customer's requests for smaller amounts needed for minor matters, even for mortgage financing.

This hiccup with your bank can occur even if you have good credit or even if your property is qualified as a security tool.

Berry Gordy, the founder of Motown Records that brought out the likes of Diana Ross, Michael Jackson, and Smokey Robinson, recognised this banking challenge when he first attempted to launch his home based record label.

So what he did, was use a sort of strip mall loan from a Detroit underground strip lending entity, and combine it with a $800 loan from his family, to launch a home based record label which would form the foundation for the largest record label in the world.

So if you are facing a bank loan challenge or you simply

need a small time funding to get your home based business firing, you can take the leap like Berry Gordy, and transform your idea into another Motown.

The good thing about a strip mall lending service is that you can get approve in less than 24hrs.

Such services will also work with you to finance loans that others banks will not want to handle.

Though the interest rates are high, you do not have to worry about having a decent credit score, or about having to provide a pile of documentation.

Loans can be granted from as little as $500, to as much as $25,000.
It can be used for anything other than a business loan (say vacation, bills consolidation, repairs, etc).

The key here is to not tell them that you are using it for a business. Because most of these services are not authorized to give you a business loan and may even deny your application if you tell them.

But either way, it is still an option that you can smartly use to help fund your home business.

Some of the companies with a good reputation in a variety of jurisdictions, can be found online, but not limited to;

www.onemainfinancial.com

or

www.springleaffinancial.com/

Loan From Family Elders

 Like Berry Gordy and his $800 loan from his family members, which transformed into a multi-million dollar enterprise at Motown, you too can consider approaching senior members of your family to aid you in your home business pursuits.

Asking a family member such as your grand parents or a senior aunt is a good idea, if they are known to have acquired a stable saving or is in possession of a stable retirement account, or has other disposable assets.

While they are sometimes hard to convince, you can get around this by showing and discussing the details of your business plans with them, while asking for their advise for success.

Explain your financial shortfalls to them, and seek out their consideration for a short term loan.

However, you should be considerate in your requests, and not try to be ridiculous by asking for an alarming sum, or an amount that may be difficult for them to consider.

If a large amount is needed it might be better to borrow from two or three senior family members, but remember to let them know that you have taken a split loan from each of them. Otherwise, you might end up in the dishonesty book, and may even be deterred from borrowing if they become aware that you are seemingly taking the same loan seeking story to each family member in secrecy.

If an agreement is necessary in writing, do not hesitate to sign it, once you are satisfied with the terms. Alternatively, you can simply offer to do a promissory note.

As a matter of caution, you should only uplift an approved loan from your senior family member when you are actually ready to use it, and for the business funding purpose that you had explained to your lender.

The fact that interest is usually forgiven on family loans, you may want to do your best to pay them back on time, which may offer you an opportunity to borrow again if your business begins to experience subsequent hiccups.

A sustained source from which you can borrow at short notice is always a better tool for any home based business, and can act as a form of financial insurance for your home based business operation.

However, while borrowing from a senior family member is a great idea, it will be best to put an agreement in place, and have two other relatives to sign as witness, as it relates to the loan.

This is because transactions of this nature can sometimes be erroneously interpreted by other relatives or law enforcement as an act of financial abuse of an elderly person.

That is to suggest that you purportedly took access to the cash of an elderly relative (by force or by their approval) without them recognizing the purpose for which you had took the cash, knowing fully well that they will be unable to prevent you from doing so, or would not had given you the cash if they understood that you was taking or supposedly borrowing or taking it from them.

Unintentionally landing yourself in such a trap may not be good for your small business reputation, even if the conflict was brief.

Therefore, it will be best for you to urge them to make a note of the loan, the amount, and the terms; much to the knowledge of at least two other family members.

In that way, the room for any future event that is contrary

your reputation will be avoided, and you will be on your way safely with the loan.

 If a yard sale is not your thing, or you prefer to get better prices for your items, as you seek to garner financial input for your home business, then eBay can also be a good choice.

Of course we are not short of eBay funding success stories, which ranges from the millions made by Matt and Amanda Clarkson, to the small business fund generation successes of Lynn Dralle, among others.

Thus I would not want to regale you with the details of these many stories for fear of your over excitement, as I am sure that you are already aware of quite a few eBay successes yourself.

Nonetheless, the bottom line is that you can surely make some extra cash for business funding on eBay if you have the goodies and an impressive advert portfolio.

To get started, you can simply go to the official eBay website (www.ebay.com), and sign up for an account, which usually takes under five minutes.

Of course, this is not just about an account, only. Its about ensuring that you have the items to feature, and for a good bidding price.

You can list almost any movable item that is legal on eBay, except items requiring special licenses such as firearm, prescription medicines etc.

However eBay is more common for customers who are shopping for electronics, gadgets, and brand name items.

So if you have cameras, expensive mobile phones, and other tech stuff, then you may be in for some quick luck.

To list an item, you can use your account control panel to add the details of the products you are selling in addition to photos of the merchandise, for visitors to see.

It is always best to use photos from the original item itself (in its current state) so that potential bidders can have a true view of the product quality.

You should also indicate the true product condition in your description, so that potential buyers will know whether there are some minor scratches, dent, or a missing charger, etc.

In this way, it will ensure that your customer is satisfied, and that your cash will eventually be released without incident from eBay.

And after a few weeks and some good business ethics, I am sure that you will be able to earn just enough to help fund your home based business ideas.

Craigslist

 If you have other local service skills or items that does not fit into eBay, then you can also try and use the free local listing service at Craigslist, and get the word out.

Miami's small business success story stalwart Danny Maynard had told the Business Week Magazine in 2012 that much of his small business funding had came from cash he had acquired via supplementary sales advisory services he was offering to locals through Craigslist.

Originally wanting to establish a herbal products store but short on cash, Danny turned to Craigslist where he list his advisory skills, and soon gain a lot of clients who used many variations of his services, which helped him to raise over $200,000 in less than a year, and just enough to open his first herbal supplements store in downtown Miami.

Within two years, Danny was able to add three more chained stores to his operations, with a worth of over three million dollars.

Like Danny, you too can take some of your skills or products to Craigslist, or even seek out people who may
already be advertising for your skills-set there.

You might be surprised at the volume of income you can start raking in via Craigslist to help fund your home business.

The good thing about Craigslist is that an account can be set up in under 5 minutes, so that you can sell your services or items at short notice.

Transactions are done locally in cash between you and the customer, and is quite similar to simply placing a newspaper advert.

Sell Your Extra Car

So you have two cars sitting in the garage right?

While it may be good to have a back up vehicle in your driveway, you may not necessarily need to use both of them, and obviously cannot drive them all at the same time.

So why don't you consider selling one off so that you can have the money to get your home based business started?

After all, if you are really confident in your business prospects then you should be able to buy a newer model sometime down the road.

Selling off the extra car can also help you to ease the burden of its insurance, and installments payments, since you can simply settle your car loan, while still having a great deal of cash to fund your home business.

Sell Your Big Boy/ Girl Toys

 When a Cleveland, Ohio mom, Nicola Dyer decided in 2011 that she will be going into a home based investment as an Amway product representative, she realized she did not have the size of funding that she would have needed to launch herself out on a grand scale.

But having confidence in her simple Amway business plans and a strong scope for profitability, she sold her son's gaming system, an extra laptop computer, a tablet, and a jet ski to raise the required sums in her bid to fund her home business.

Overtime, she was able to successfully affect her business operations, and pay off a previously troubled mortgage, while restoring a new jet ski, and a new gaming system for her son, as her expanding sales business continued to rake in over $400,000 per year.

Like Nicola, many of us should consider trading off our big toys for cash, if we are really serious and confident about our impending investment.

As such, it may be best to simply sell off some of our luxury goods such as overpriced lawn mowers, boats, motorcycle, and other hardly used items to raise quick cash to fund your home business initiatives.

Use Your Disability Insurance

 Though this may not apply to all of us, you may be able to gather funding for your home based business by utilizing the money from your disability insurance.

Of course, this may depend upon the size and nature of your insurance payout. But if from the seven types of disability insurance in play today, you was able to pull in a reasonably sized check whether in one tranche or by a periodic payment system, you can consider using some of that cash to fund your home business and get yourself on the road to a stable income.

If you are not sure that this will be worth it, well then you may need to consider the history of the world's third richest rapper; Master P, whose $350 million empire had given him a space in Forbes Magazine.

This is a man who had pulled himself out of one of the roughest and poorest ghettos in New York city, by launching a now globally successful business by using a portion of a $10,000 insurance settlement check, to open a record retail shop.

And if Master P. could have achieved this from a $10,000 medical malpractice (disability) insurance check, who is to say that you can't turn yours into a driving force for your home based business.

Use Your Unemployment Check

 Just like your medical insurance check, you can use your unemployment benefit check to aid in the funding of your home base business.

While a check of this nature may not be big in size, the story of the Maryland millionaire Calvin Benn should serve as an example that even a $120 benefit check can help you to build an online business empire.

Similarly, you can even bet on the most recent story of Jason Glaspey, the owner of www.paleoplan.com, who now earns around $5,000 per month, after using about $100 from his unemployment check to kick start his home based Paleo plan website.

Using the same methodology, anyone of us can take a chip out of our unemployment benefits check and be on the road to a successful home based business, which might cost nothing more than a cheap tablet computer.

To obtain an unemployment benefit check, you may need to check and ensure that you satisfies the eligibility requirements for this concession.

Once you are past that, then you can file an unemployment claim online or in person with the appropriate authorities.

If your claim is approved, you can then keep filing on a weekly basis, and soon your checks will start flowing in the mail.

With the check in your hands, you can still eat a little while getting your home based business off of the ground.

Sell Your Food Stamps

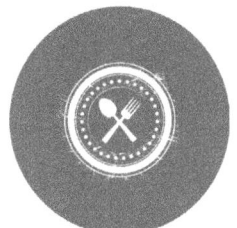 When the founder of WhatsApp, Jan Koum, sold his company to Facebook for $19 billion in early 2014, he signed all of the the paperwork at the front entrance of a welfare office where he and his family used to go to collect food stamps.

But of more significance, it was the revenue earned from his food stamps, that had made him $19 billion richer from an initially seemingly insignificant internet user's App business that he had started from his run down home.

To the millions of news readers and hundreds of news casters, it was a strange addition to the list of many famous others such as the Democratic state senator Barbara Buono, and super star Bruce Springsteen who had also built their careers from selling food stamps.

Considered by many to be immoral, and certainly against the law, you in the same way as Jan Koum can also consider selling your food stamps to generate cash.

Though practiced by many in the lower income earning bracket, revenue from your food stamp can certainly help you to get your home base business started, and maybe make you the next internet billionaire like Jan.

Pawn The Title Of Your Car

 If you are really pressed for some quick funding, then one of the best option may be to visit a mart that would accept the pawned title of your car.

These types of loans are usually processed within a day or two, and may not require any credit check, but is maximize at thirty days at a time, which can be extended for a repeated thirty days, on a low interest rate.

To raise funds via this channel, and apart from being in possession of a car, you must satisfy a listing of general requirements, which entails that; -

(1) **the vehicle is in good condition;** -- The average lender would require that your vehicle is in a good condition.This means that there should be no extensive body damage and no other disqualifying elements such as a troubled engine or transmission issues.

Additionally,the car must not have any general mechanical problems or excessive rust, and must pass all emission tests,in addition to being road worthy.

(2) you provide ID and age verification: -- In all instances, you as the borrower must prove that you are at least eighteen years or older via a valid state identification or a drivers license.

(3) The vehicle must be owned free of any debts: -- Among the qualifying requirements for an auto loan,you may have to satisfy the lender that the car or its title id is free from any additional debt or circumstances that can make it difficult for the lender to repossess the vehicle if there is a default on repayment.

(4) You provide employment and income requirements; -- While the lender may not look at your credit rating,they may want to ensure that you have means and options to repay the loan.Therefore you may need to provide some sort of proof that you are gaining a lawful income.

This can range from a job letter,a telephone reference,or any justification to the lender during the interview that you are capable of repaying the loan.

(5) You agree to the loan terms and rollovers; -- In order to preserve the legality of the loan you as the borrower will have to agree to an established loan period, which is usually short, and establishes all of the required terms for rollovers, contingencies ,and arrangements for defaulting situations.

Upon approval, you are generally required to turn over a second set of keys and the title of your car, before the cash is handed over.

The good thing about this category of loan, is that you will still be able to enjoy the use of your car, unless you are in extreme default.

In this way, you will be able to pick up some quick cash, and fund your home base business without the hiccups.

Pawn Your Junk

There is a modern word of wisdom which denotes that one man's junk is another man's luxury.

An April 2014 featured content on CNN emphasize just this when it published an extraction from the popular ebook, *Red Paper Clip*, in which the story of Canadian blogger Kyle McDonald, (*who reached financial stardom after making a fortune from selling his junk items*), was featured.

Originally, Kyle was struggling from a lack of income, and had needed funding for his small home based blogging business.

Being acutely cash strapped, he turned to his collection of junk and had them properly appraised before taking them to the pawn shop.

Interestingly, he raised quite a few thousand dollars from nearly every piece of junk ,starting from a red paper clip to a 1970's sweater.

With over $13,000 in reward loitering in his hands, funding his home based business became a breeze.

Since then, Kyle has become an inspiration for most home based business owners, who are struggling for adequate funding for their home based business operation.

Similarly, across the border in the United States, a struggling jobless dad, Adrian Ankovic, did not know where to turn or who to turn to after deciding that he need to set up an internet based business, which he perceives to be capable of raking in some big earnings.

With his credit in limbo, and finding it difficult to secure a loan, he simply resorted to pawning two rings, a large collection of CD's, and other equipment to a Yonkers New York pawnbroker.

Leaving their establishment with $1,480 in cash, he returned home and began to engage in an online brokerage system where he helped buyers online to source a specific product by taking their orders, sourcing the product on eBay or a similar place and then resell it to the customer for the price that they had desired to pay.

After making an initial $150 profit on the first day, Adrian successfully drove that home based business operation to a mega $600,000 a year internet brokerage entity.

Similarly, if you can seek out a collection of your items, such as electronic devices, CD's, Jewellery, gaming systems, guns, etc, you can take them to the pawn shop and fetch yourself a hefty sum that may more than likely be good enough to give your home based business the starting steps that it needs.

Cook For People

Maybe you haven't figured it out yet, but there are many people out there who don't know how to cook.

From elderly people, working parents, people who don't know to cook, lazy people, health conscious people, busy people,rich people, and the list goes on and on.

There is always someone somewhere who needs a cooking service. So if you are a good cook, then another easy revenue earner is to offer to cook for a few busy couples or families in your neighborhood or even friends who lives across town, for a fee.

To stand out, you should first come up with a list of menu ideas that you think would serve the culinary interest of your community.

If you are living in an area that is swollen with business professionals, then you may need to specifically cater to their appetite by offering up a series of healthy meals that they can eat on the go.

On the other hand, if you are in a family knitted neighborhood then you may have to prepare family meals that the average mom or dad can modify or later reheat in the oven at their convenience.

But generally, your clients will usually be working professionals, such as lawyers, doctors, accountants, bankers, etc.

Cooking up meals for these professionals and their families is usually not a whole day task, and will certainly bring you some big dollars to get your home based business started.

Former Desperate Housewives star Eva Longoria use to cook for her friends for a fee, and also once worked part time at a Wendy's restaurant where she assisted in the cooking processes, and later took on other tasks in other to raise cash to fund her drama career upliftment, while attending high school.

So regardless of what your home based business interest may be, a little cooking service for professionals around the neighborhood can certainly do you some financial good.

Reverse Mortgage

 It is not unusual for us to be in a position where we are in need of funding to start a home based business but do not want to be straddled in any way with the responsibility of repaying a mortgage, or having to lose the home in default.

In such a case, it will be best to fund the business with a reverse mortgage if our intention is to use our home as collateral, without the need for immediate or any repayments, or having to confront the risk of being thrown into the streets.

If we take the case of the immigrant owner of *Basket Delights* in Brooklyn, New York, we may recollect her explained challenges in a MSN feature where she spoke of her plight of being stuck in a mortgage hole back in 2005, and had almost no other piece of asset to acquire some funding for her home based baking business that was in its planning phase.

But interestingly she found a way out by taking a rather tough decision to refinance her mortgage, and redirect some of her cash to fund her home based business, while cutting back on certain existing expenses.

Four years later, her home was free from mortgage, and her business was blooming with a growing profit of around $300,000 per year. In 2012, she was also able to open two more stores in her native country of Barbados, and a smaller branch in Grenada.

In the same way, you can take a serious look at doing a reverse mortgage, and consider money saving steps such as car pooling, savings digging, and other measures that will lower your expenses while creating an avenue for you to raise the funds to get your home based business moving apace.

The main advantage of a reverse mortgage is centered on the fact that your credit would not be relevant, and is often unchecked, since the borrower will not need to make any payments.

This is because your home will serve as collateral, and must be sold in the future in order to repay the mortgage whenever you are deceased. However, there is usually an option for the heirs of the estate to repay the mortgage and take possession of the property.

A reverse mortgage will ensure that you secure the finance to start your home based business without worrying about actually paying it back.

It may also be the most suitable option for retirees or seniors who are in need of large scale financing to launch a home based business that might turned into a family inheritance after several years of hard work and revolving investment.

Borrow All From Family

 When bank loans and other credit options are dried up, the next best option is to borrow a collective loan from your family (and even close friends).

But even though borrowing from family and friends can be an easy means of getting inexpensive financing for your home based business, it can also turn into a recipe for disaster that can lead to family disputes, sad breakdowns in relationships and even legal wranglings.

So if you are going to borrow from your family, still consider it as a business transaction, and try not to borrow more than that family member can afford to lose.

However, before you attempt to borrow, first make your own true assessment as to which group of family members will be more inclined to help you, or may rather be glad to see you succeed at something.

Once you have identified the few that are most likely to be supportive, you should first approach them by introducing them to your home based business idea, and allow the entire concept to favorably sink in to their vision.

Do not discuss borrowing from them immediately at the time you have shared your idea, because a person who have not had the opportunity to properly reflect on something would most likely feeled pushed, and may most likely say no to you.

Therefore, you should simply keep the discussion to the level of just making them excited about your home based business prospects.

After about two weeks or so thereafter, you should contact them again, and let them know that you wish to have an important meeting with them regarding the home business initiative that you had shared with them a few weeks before.

Try not to force their schedule, and instead let them take the lead in giving you a time that is convenient to them.

The reason behind letting them set the meeting schedule is based upon the fact that a potential lender can become irritable if you pressed them too much to be available on your time.

This might be an early turn off that you may want to avoid.

But once they set a mutually convenient schedule, then it may be time for you to make the best of the meeting.

Ensure that you show them your business plan, and discuss your business prospects in detail in a bid to win their support.

Overall, seeking financial help from your family members, your in laws and close friends is not a bad choice. But again, please ensure that you treat it like any other respected business transaction.

Borrow All From A Stranger

 Approaching strangers for a business loan is not a bad task, but should be treated with the same level of respect as a standard loan from a banking institution.

Strangers does not mean someone passing on the street or someone whom you have never met.

It means, financially sound individuals that your spouse or a close friend may know, someone at the gym, or someone you interfaced with at a business meeting.

Strangers would not necessarily deny you because you are technically a stranger too.

After all, many successful global business enterprises started off with loans from strangers, who never regretted helping to make those businesses what they are today.

A typical example is the founder of Starbucks; Mr. Howard D. Schultz, who had to borrow monies from two of his wife's friends, and his family doctor in order to open his first coffee business enterprise, which resulted in him becoming one of the richest men in America, according to Forbes magazine.

Therefore, if you can develop the charisma and will spirit of Howard Schultz, then you can certainly convince some strangers to help you to get your home based business off of the ground.

Referral Business

 Another way of adding monies to your home business funding coffers is to sign up for referrals.

Historically, referrals has always been a great way to make from as little as $20 to as much as $2,000 in one month.

Some of the best places to seek out referral cash is at medium and small size city businesses, car dealers, community banks, bail court brokers, HVAC companies, and real estate agents.

The above collection of entities would usually pay varying sums to you for referring active clients to them, or for providing them with clients who have turned out to be buying customers.

One of the things to keep in mind is that most local business owners are always generally willing to give you money to help them.

At the same time, you must be mindful of the businesses that you decides to refer people to.

After all, referrals can have its disadvantages for you if you have been referring members of your community to illegal business operations, get rich quick schemes, and other categories of businesses that are not above board, or that can result in legal implications for you later in life.

Some of the more risky categories of referrals to work for are generally online business operations without a widely known public record that confirms their genuine existence, some virtual businesses, no-sample product referral businesses, long distance sign up referrals businesses, loan schemes, and operations that makes it difficult for you to liaise with someone in person at a real address or on a publicly vetted phone number.

Therefore, you must carefully assess the businesses for which you are about to work for, and ensure that what they are asking you to do is not putting you at a personal risk with the law or your reputation.

For example, do not allow a business entity to let you advertise a product by referral for $2, and when the customer gets there, the staff says its $3.

These occurrences can impact your reputation and the reputation of your future home based business since people would have long lost their confidence in your words.

But putting all of that aside, working for a reputable company as a referrer can certainly make a positive impact on savings to fund your home based business.

In general, working part time as a referrer with a reputable establishment would also generate goodwill with business owners who may more than likely be willing to aid your home business funding needs, or simply allow you to have them as a viable customer.

As a matter of fact you should tell them why you are helping them, so that they may know that you are starting a Home business, and need their help too.

In such a case, the business owner will be more inclined to be your number one money generating medium, by extending more rewarding tasks to you.

Get Sponsored By A Sponsor

 Sometimes the easiest way out of your home business funding struggle is to simply seek out a sponsor.

Thought this is a rare feat, it is never an impossibility.

Approaching a sponsor means that you will also have to share your business plans, ideas, and developmental strategies in order to convince them to support you.

Sponsors generally like to weigh the benefit of their sponsorship, by evaluating whether what you are about to do may be profitable in their view, may benefit your community, or may benefit a grouping of people as a whole.

As a matter of inducement, you can let your sponsor know that you are willing to lodge any piece of asset that can assure them that you are willing to repay what they have contributed.

This way you may have a firmer hold on a sponsorship possibility, while the sponsor will become confident that the risk will be minimal.

But the best teaser in this (if its a company owner) is to tell your sponsor that you are willing to give back a percentage of your profits to any just cause in the community for a period of one year (until the sponsored amount is exhausted), and will repeatedly give the sponsor credit as the facilitator of each donation.

This would help your sponsor to appreciate your consideration for their investment and your community.

And if you are lucky enough, then you should soon be able to get your home based business off the ground with a sponsorship check.

Start A Fiverr

 Fiverr is basically a global online market place where people sell services to cheap buyers from as little as five dollars, and upward.

You can either charge someone for a service such as writing a 400 word article for one gig (which is equivalent to $5), or designing a poster for three gigs (which is $5 x 3).

Therefore, you can earn from as little as five dollars to as much as $500 for every business service that you delivers to a client on Fiverr.

Since, it requires no credit check, offers a three minutes sign up ritual, and directly deposits your earnings into your local bank account, *Fiverr.com* may offer you a good option to pick up some extra cash to fund your home based business.

All you will require is an internet connected computer, and some time to interface with potential buyers via the website.

According to *usnews.com*, fiverr users earns a lot of money even sometimes more than traditional 9 to 5 workers.

Using an example, they quoted Fiverr's user Mark Mason, a semi-retired publicist from Chicago, who earns somewhere between $150 to $300 per day on Fiverr, with only three to four hours of input daily.

So if you take up a task on F*iverr.com*, who knows what your daily income for your home business funding can be.

Get A Sus- Or A Partner

According to the notable, International Business Times, and Forbes Magazine Partnerships are often a very good way to move an entire business enterprise forward, and may indeed be as good enough for home base businesses where cash flow for the start up is a problem.

You can be the most educated entrepreneur , who can single-handily establish your own home based business venture from the ground up, but that does not necessarily means that you should do so.

Collaborating with a partner for your home based business can surprisingly save you from spending all of the required funding for the entity while providing you with an extra mind and extra hand to make the venture to sustain itself.

Many successful partnerships were started as home based entities and propelled into multimillion dollar operations without much expense to either partner.

Instagram may be an ideal example of a home based partnership that has quickly evolved into a billionaire venture without the partner having to make too much sacrifices.

Another extension to this is to simply embed yourself in a partnership financing club where ten or twelve people can borrow from each other.

This may be informally similar to a lending club without the credit requirements , or having to endure any credit checks.

This practice is more often accepted as a lending format for people from other countries like the Caribbean or Latin America, and is made up of a close network of family or friends.

In the same way, you can use your *sus* loan to fund your home based business operation without involving a co-partner, if you are not too keen on partnerships or the business is too small to accommodate a co-owner.

Cash In Stocks Options.

 Depending on where you work or had previously worked, you might be in possession of stocks which were offered up to you by your employer, which is in essence, some holding shares of the company's stock.

If you are in possession of such stocks then you can examine the option of cashing in your stock for cash.

For example, Kathy Denning, an Albany , New York internet shopping broker was struggling back in 2010 to finance the establishment of her home based business enterprise.

And as part of her efforts to raise funds, she and her husband turned to a total of 1,000 stocks that they were holding in a company, with which one spouse still worked.

Back in 2008, they had bought a cash-based call option contract with a strike price of $55.

At the time that Kathy was in need of cash in 2010, the stock was valued at $60 per share. This means that a collection of one thousand shares will have a net value of $5,000 (60 minus 55 x 1000).

Rather than selling off her stock, she cashed in on her investment and received a $5,000 check which she used to acquire additional tools to fund her home based business initiative.

In a similar fashion, you can turn to cashing in your stock options like Kathy (or even ask your spouse or relative to cash in theirs) so that you can get the required financing for your home based business establishment.

Hard Money Lender

Hard money lenders are a selection of lending companies that offers a unique type of real-estate backed loans.

They practically lends short-term capital of a certain amount , based on the value of the real estate that is acting as the collateral.

The fees are generally high and admittedly, the risk is high, but you will usually get the money if you have real estate holdings.

However, if you are one who is not too keen about taking up the Hard Money Lender route, then there are other less-risks options that you can consider, without the compulsory use of your existing real estate.

An option to this may be to work out a similar arrangement with your house of worship, since they can loan you the money if you are in good standing, or simply borrow from your spouse business, or one of your other businesses (if any), to fund your new home based business.

Sell Your Holiday Gifts

 When *Mc Donalds* told its employees back in 2013 that a good way to make some extra cash is to simply sell off those holiday gifts to earn additional money, most people felt that their advise was an old, and maybe ridiculous one.

After all, selling things generates income, and can aid us in more ways than we can expect during our times of financial need.

In reality, most of us accumulate a lot of stuff that we do not need during the holidays.

Sometimes we have too much of gifts and presents from a succession of holidays or at various intervals, but practically has no need or real use for them

This can range from well intentioned but bad-choice gifts, items that were bought during a bargain that we could not have resisted, items bought on impulse, or unwanted items that was gifted to you.

For example, you may have had accepted a sweater or a

gadget from your favourite aunt as a gift during the holidays but did not rejected it because it would have been unethical for you o do so.

However, it is all now sitting in your closet unopened and unused, but harboring a lot of dusts while taking up needed space.

This simply occurs because a lot us end up hoarding unwanted gifts repeatedly over various holiday seasons, and usually would not do anything about it.

Interestingly, a long gone survey by *Purolator* found that almost 65% of north Americans kept holiday gifts that they do not like, had outgrown, or had failed to use for varying reasons.

If you fit into this bill, then it will be a good idea to gather up all of your intact holiday gifts, and make a sale on eBay or any other auction site.

I am sure that you will rake in some sizable cash that can make a difference in your quest to fund your home based business project.

Ask Your Family For A Gift Of Money.

 If you are the type of person that is fortunate to get lots of gifts for a birthday or celebration from family members, then it will be best for you to nicely request the cash equivalent as a gifts, rather than a gift item itself.

Take a leaf out of the book of Houston tea shop owner, Jaqueline May, who took a similar initiative and was able to raise more than $14,000 by frankly spilling her need for cash gifts to family and friends.

She was then able to successfully launch her home based business in 2012, which has now expanded into a thriving and favourite downtown Houston health food and tea shop.

Her advise to newbies is to let your family and friends know that you are trying to launch a home based business and is working hard on finance.

After a few days or so, or rather when a seasonal gift period is coming up, you should nicely call each one of them up and let them know that you would really appreciate it if they can consider a small cash gift since you would really like to turn your gifts into monetary contributions to your home based business.

According to Jackie (as she is sometimes called) this way of gathering home based funding is a good thing because it does not require you to pay back anything, and can be very effective around major holiday periods, and your birthday.

Use Your Wedding Gifts.

 If you just got married there is a likelihood that some of that cash gifts and the other gift sets may still be hanging around in your home.

Interestingly, you can sell your wedding gifts to raise money to fund your emerging home based business.

And if you think that it is a bad idea, then the thousands who did it before you do not think so.

One of the most touching cases of such nature is Benon Lugya, who happens to be one of the richest men on the African continent.

Born in Uganda, Mr. Benon Lugya's life memoirs explains how he sold off his wedding gifts to start a home business, which has now evolved into the largest food processing firm in East Africa.

The multimillionaire has repeatedly credited the sale of his wedding gift as the leading funding source for his now multimillion dollar business, *Maganjo Grain Millers*.

My simple take on this is that if Benon Lugya could have

done it from the sale of his wedding gifts, so can you.

Therefore, if you still have much of your gifts hanging around, then it is time for you to push them off on eBay, and get your home based business up and running.

Take The Gifts Back From The Baby Shower.

 If you just had a baby shower and there is a bunch of valuable left over gifts, there is no harm in you wanting to return them in order to raise cash.

The best approach to this is to talk with your friends and relatives who brought baby shower gifts, and let them know that you are starting a home base business that you know will benefit the upbringing of your child.

Nonetheless, since you are short on cash to start the business, you have decided to return some of the gifts in anticipation of getting a cash refund.

However, you are kindly asking for their support and understanding, in as much that you would have appreciate them letting you have the receipt to facilitate the smooth return of the gift, for cash.

On the other hand, if they are not approachable, you might as well take the baby shower items to eBay. I am sure that they will be some eager buyers who would bargain with you there, and pay you handsomely. So either way, you should be able to rake in some funds from your baby shower left overs, and effectively fund your home base business.

Use "will work for food sign" ---*say "starting a home business---bad credit---please help"*

 Of course you may have to put some of your ego aside, but people will naturally be more inclined to help those that help themselves, even more often than they would help a charity.

Therefore, you can indicate on a sign that you are starting a home based business, and is willing to do odd jobs or help out anyone who may need a genuine service, so that you can raise cash to start your project.

As mentioned before, you may have to put your ego aside, and get over your thinking that people you know will be ashamed of your actions.

After all, you are still trying to raise money in an honest way.

Donate Your Hair For Cash

 On the 21st March, 2012, the UK Mail Online newspaper ran an article about an emerging home business owner name Amanda Golding.

The story was based upon the fact that Amanda was struggling for cash to get her home based business idea off the ground, and had also needed money to take care of her two year old son.

But after failing to get a loan or proper financial input from anywhere else, she decided to join a long list of women who had decided to sell their hair for cash.

And in less than a week, Amanda sold off her thick natural blonde locks of about three feet, and had almost $1,000 in her possession to fund her home business and help take care of her son.

Today, her initiative had paid off, as she now has a flourishing business operation, thanks to her hair.

Therefore, if you are similarly in a cash strap position, you can turn to selling your hair, which can rake in between $400 to $4,000 according to *Marlys Fladeland*, who runs one of the largest hair sale websites in the United States at *Hairwork.com*.

With that kind of money, you can safely fund your home based business, depending on its budget.

Donate Your Blood Plasma For Cash

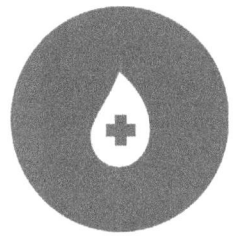 Donating that clear yellowish fluid that is used to transport all of the energies around our body is a sure and simple way to earn some extra cash to fund your home based business drive.

All you have to do is ensure that you fit the requirements and head off to the nearest plasma collection center or blood bank, as they are called.

There are literally hundreds of blood banks all over the world, with a large concentration of them being in North America and Europe.

Some of these blood banks operates directly out of hospitals, while others are situated at specialize plasma collection centers.

Since there is a continuous need for various blood types at practically every medical institutions; - brokers and hospitals alike are always willing to compensate donors handsomely, for their blood plasma.

As a primary requirement, you must be healthy, be physically fit, weight in proportion to your height (with a minium weight of 100 pounds), be at least 18 years of age, and have your ID to prove it.

It is also important that you did not had any piercings, tattoo work done or unprotected and risky sex during the previous three months, as the entity must screen you, and will reject your candidacy if you are HIV positive or is infected with some other STD or communicable disease.

So if you think that you can satisfy all of the requirements, then it should be ok for you to head off to the plasma.

But before heading off to sell your plasma, it is important that you consider taking lots of water or any related non-alcoholic beverage, and eat a meal that is rich in protein, preferably at least three hours before the procedure.

After all, drinking a great deal of water beforehand will help your blood to move much faster through the body, thus making the process a much faster and easier one, while keeping you hydrated after the procedure.

On the other hand, your plasma contains most of the protein in your blood, and can result in you feeling very weak and tired after the procedure, unless you were fed a protein embedded meal.

But as explained before; - if you are free of diseases, free from substance abuse, and can pass a basic medical check up, then you should consider being a regular blood plasma donor, and you should be able to earn a regular tranche of cash to put towards your home based business prospects.

Donate To A Sperm Bank

 With the advancement of medical technology, a wife with an infertile husband, a lesbian partner, or even a single professional woman, can seek redress at a sperm bank by utilizing donated sperm from a fertile and usually anonymous male.

So, for a male struggling to fund his home business idea (or a wife needing cash and consented to her husband donating his sperm) resorting to a sperm bank and getting paid for your sperm can be a fair and simple option.

Of course, you would have had to satisfy a medical check up so as to ensure that you are healthy, and have fertile sperm for donation.

Once you are past that test, then you will be able to get cash from the sperm bank for your sperm.

Cash is generally paid right away, and can be between a low and a high range depending on the genetic quality, client demand, and health level of your sperm.

Nonetheless, you should be able to pull in some bits of cash to help fund your home based business dreams.

Donate Your Eggs

 For a price tag of $8,000, Alexis, a University of Denver student, agreed to donate her eggs, after satisfying medical professionals and her recipient that she is the ideal candidate for their cause.

According to Alexis, she had needed the money to fund a home based retail business in the area of internet marketing and cosmetic distribution.

Admitting that it is not necessarily a simple process to please the recipient, Alexis explained that the first step is usually a questionnaire that queries your name, your age, whether you have a college degree, if you smoke, if you were ever tested positive for any sexually transmitted disease, how many partners you have slept with, and so on.

Once you are past that assessment, a medical evaluations will be done, followed by a specific examination to analyze the quality and genetic compatibility of your eggs.

At this stage, you will usually be given about 50% of the egg donor fee, which can usually be somewhere between

$2000 to $5,000, depending on the preliminary agreement that you may have with the egg recipient.

However, once all is well, the process usually takes between two weeks to a month to be completed, and you should be walking away with a big check at the end of it all.

Like Alexis, you can use the large payout to fund your home based business.

Use Your Tax Refund

 Of course there is a season that we call tax season. It is the time when those tax refund checks will start finding their way into our mailbox.

And if you are like Marvin Briggs, the owner of the leading Caribbean Sea food restaurant on Nostrand Avenue in New York, then you would realize the impact a tax refund check can have on the growth of a home based business.

Marvin was struggling to maintain a family kitchen that his mom had died and left as a *de facto* inheritance on a lower floor apartment in Brooklyn.

The family kitchen use to basically provide cheap meals for about 60 to 70 persons in their environs per day.

But in a matter of months the business began to take a downward spiral, as customers began to shift away to other food suppliers.

And before he knew it, the family kitchen was no more.

But being determined to relaunch the family's home based business entity Marvin kept his focused on sourcing cash, but did not reached his required sum until he received a tax refund check in the mail for $1,300.

From then, the rest was history.

With the tax refund, Marvin was able to refinance the home based business, and earned enough to buy out a space on Nostrand avenue in 2012, to open the first branch outside of his home, followed by two more branches in Manhattan during 2013.

Like Marvin, you can take your tax refund check, and let your home based business become a part of business development history.

Borrow Against Your Future Tax Return.

 Refund Anticipation Loans (RALs) or tax return loans is a funding process where you use your anticipated tax return as the collateral for a loan, but which usually comes with a high interest rate.

If you have a stable and long term arrangement with a Tax Consultancy, who may be aware of your usual annual income, then it would be a good idea to borrow from your tax consultant directly or under the auspices of the firm.

Explain thoroughly to them that you are venturing into a home based business, and is short on cash to get it started, but is seeking to borrow against your anticipated tax return.

Let them have a look at your business plan, and your budgetary statements, while letting them know that you are also open to their advise and guidance. This will usually make them feel more attached to what you are doing.

And before you know it, you might be marching to the bank with a check for the budgeted amount from your tax consultant.

However, you should be aware that the interest effect date for refund anticipation loans began from the moment you are handed the check, and will be calculated for every month that your tax return earnings are delayed.

Therefore, you must be mindful that it could take months for a tax return to process, and quite some time for you to receive your check.

But if you are mindful of the possible interest charging circumstances, then this is certainly a good way to go, as you seek to fund your home based business ideas.

Sell A Farm Animal Or Farm Implement.

 Like other assets that you would have had for disposal around the house, you can also seek out other marketable cash earners such as a farm animal if you have any, or even any agricultural hardware or farm machinery that you may have no use for.

To avoid this from being a too tedious task, it would be best to post a free ad online, or contact other farmers or likeminded individuals (in your area) whose routine may have dictate their need for the equipment and/or animals that you wish to sell.

Once you find a potential buyer or two, then remember to let them know the reason why you are selling the equipment. They might be more than willing to buy out your farming equipment, in a bid to support your efforts to fund your emerging home based business.

If you are focusing on selling a farm animal such as a duck, a ferret or a turkey, then you certainly cannot use certain sites such as eBay to sell it.

At best, you may want to try a free option on Craigslist, which may most likely attract a reasonable lot of local buyers.

For a start, when posting your ad on Craigslist, always ensure that you include a picture and the price of whatever animal you are selling.
This will usually help interested parties to determine whether they are interested in what you are selling or not.

But once your ad is live, you can expect responses from different type of people; which ranges from kids calling about the duck without their parents permission, time wasters who are not really interested, scammers who are looking to dupe you, and of course folks who are genuinely interested in your sale.

However, at the end the day, there will be enough legitimate callers to make your animal sale efforts a positive experience.

Refinance The House On A Different Plan And Take Out Some Cash

Refinancing is the method used to obtain a new mortgage in a bid to reduce their monthly payments, change mortgage companies, lower their interest rates, secure cash to start a new business, or get cash for large purchases.

Just like a reverse mortgage, you can also take refinancing steps aimed at obtaining finance via a financial institution for business purposes.

Once your credit score is favorable, you should not have any trouble getting your bank to refinance your mortgage or even another banking institution to do so.

However, depending on the purpose that you had given to the bank, you must ensure that you can have access to the refinancing cash, so that you can easily chip off a small sum of it to fund your home based business.

Borrow From Life Insurance Policy

After a certain number of contributions, some life insurance policies would allow you to borrow a loan against it, for various reasons.

For example, Nicola Selman the proud owner of *Nic's Caribbean Scents* , a two storied business that is now nested on the outskirts of Orlando, Florida, had initially decided to start a home based business that caters for the import and community retail of scented oils and flowers from the Caribbean, back in 2009.

However, for a lack of finance, Nicola and her spouse were unable to raise enough funds to effectively start the business in their garage.

So after trying different options that was not forthcoming, she and her spouse decided to turn to their insurer for help.

To their surprise, they learnt that they could have taken a loan against their respective life policy that they had taken out with their insurer.

After receiving a $12,000 loan, Nick proceeded to fulfill her home based business needs, which subsequently blossom into a large scale business that is now run from a large two story building that they had bought after two years of continued progress.

Now making an average of $250,000 per year, Mrs. Selman told the *Business Insider* that borrowing monies from your life insurance to fund a home business is not necessarily a bad choice if you are discipline and certain about what you are getting into.

You can similarly approach your life insurer for a loan to fund your home business if your policy type permits this.

You should first inquire from your insurer about this, because individual insurance policies may vary. For example universal life, whole life, and variable life insurance policies generally have cash values. But on the other hand, term life policies generally do not have a cash value.; which means you would not be able to borrow on that type of policy.

But assuming that your policy permits borrowing, then you certainly have another solid option that can fund your home based business plans.

Sell Your Timeshare

 If you own timeshare on a good vacation property, and is seeking to raise funds for your home business without wanting to borrow from anyone, then it will be smart for you to simply sell off your timeshare.

While getting into a timeshare is easy, it might not necessarily be so easy to get out.

You should first examine the particulars of your timeshare contract, since your timeshare company would have had established rules governing the resale of your timeshare.

There are generally two ways to sell your timeshare.

You can simply choose to sell it privately to another person who would have responded to an online advert for the real estate, or you can sell it via the timeshare organization from whom you had originally bought it from; though you may loose up to 40% off of your investment this way.

Once a sale has been effected, you will usually have to pay a transfer fee, in addition to seeking the approval from a

Timeshare Committee (if any is associated with the property).

Nonetheless, if you have the patience, selling your timeshare can bring you thousands of dollars and even large real estate profits depending on the resale market value of your timeshare investment at that time.

You can then use the income from your sold timeshare to launch your home based business.

Have A Fish Fry

As a general rule, entertainment and an outdoor food hang out is always a fun way to make some money.

Therefore, offering up some delicacies and a little entertainment for two hundred or so revelers isn't a bad way to pull in some needed income to fund your home based business initiative.

If you do a fish fry on a Saturday or Sunday, you should be able to attract a greater share of supporters, unlike if you had done it on other days.

While advertising efforts for this does not have to be extensive, it will still be a good idea to do some flyers, and set up an event on Facebook so that your friends can be urged to come, while spreading the word to their friends too.

At an average of $8 per plate for a fish fry, and some additional spending by patrons on drinks, you should be able to rake in somewhere between $1,000 to $2,000 depending on the number of supporters that came to your event.

The revenue from such an event, no matter how small, can certainly go a long way in helping you to make your home based business efforts a reality.

Charity Walk

Warming up to a community charity and making plans for a funding walk is definitely a great idea.

You can discuss and agree with the charity to give them 50% of all the funds raised, while being allowed to retain the other 50% which is intended to fund the launching of your home business.

Planning a charity walk can also help to develop goodwill between yourself and the community, and create a trusted relationship for future charitable and social events.

Out of caution however, it would be best to collaborate with a smaller charity than to try to make the walking arrangement with a large one.

This is because smaller charities tends to better support this sort of initiative, rather than larger ones that already have an establish donor community in any case, and may not be tolerant of a 50-50 venture of such nature with a private person.

Once you get an endorsement from the desired charitable organization to organize the walk, you should plan a very good day for the event, while taking weather patterns, the walking route, and any needed permits into consideration.

With the necessary clearance in place from the authorities, you should then write up a special guest list, and dispatch official invitations to each person, urging them to support the walk.

After that, you, the charitable organization, and some of your special guests should embark on a publicity campaign by notifying the media of your plans and businesses that runs along the route of your walk.

In that way, you can gain the necessary publicity, and material support, on the date of the event.

So with proper planning, coordination and publicity, your charitable event should aid in bringing you a reasonable sum of cash to support your home base business dreams.

Rent Out One Of Your Rooms/ Take a Boarder

 Renting out a room in your home or facilitating a boarder to lodge at your place is an initiative that is sure to bring in some needed cash to fund your home business.

According to Forbes Magazine, property rentals generally accounts for the greater share of the real estate business, and brings in billions of dollars annually in revenue.

So if you want to cash in on the continued demand for rented space and accommodation, then you should seriously consider renting out one of your rooms (as a home stay service) to a vacationing couple or to a student who might be looking for reasonably priced boarding.

To get clients, simply post some free adverts on a few popular tourist sites (that is confine to your community) such as the local page of *tripadvisor.com*, etc.

Additionally, it may be very important for you to also place notices on the notice boards of neighboring universities, in addition to various websites that lists student accommodations.

Renting your room to visitors can bring in anywhere between $500 to $1,500 per month, depending on your visitors pattern.

Sell Your Crafts

 Many people tend to do craft as a hobby, but do you know that there is always a global demand for craftwork in all of its formats.

If you are craft minded and have the skills and patience, then it is definitely a good idea to make some simple craftwork and sell to people in your community, who may be more than willing to support your skills.

For a start, you do not need to make any major investments, and can simply recycle lots of craft-friendly stuff, which you can design and sell at any flea market.

To make your craft sales a true revenue earner, you should make an internet search and get a grasp on current craft trends, their pricing range and whether they fall within your design skills.

Pay close attention to color sets, new themes, and designs that are in continuous demand.

Once you have agreed on the patterns and items that you will make for sale, you should go ahead and design some samples, take some photos and start a marketing campaign via Facebook, Twitter, Instagram, Pinterest, and other social networks where you have a large volume of friends, and potential buyers in your community.

From there, you can start putting your craft making skills to task.

This skill-set will certainly bring in much needed cash to fund your home based business plans.

Sell Your kittens or Puppies

Who doesn't need a cute puppy or a curly kitten to embrace their feet.

Social and veterinary studies have shown that people would more easily buy a puppy or kitten as their pet than any other animal. And in some instances, they may be inclined to pay some hefty sums for a desirable one.

So if you have some wonderful kittens or some adorable puppies, and you are short on investment cash for your home based business, then it is time to consider selling some of them off to raise funds.

To get an early market, simply post pictures of the pets (you are selling) on your Facebook feed, Instagram, Pinterest or similar social sharing sites and let everyone know that they are up for sale.

The cash returns from your pet sales may have well worth the sacrifice to make your home business funding a reality.

Clean House

 In a 2009 interview on Yahoo Small Business, Jenna Oakley of Denver, Colorado, shared her experience on how she generated cash for her home based business idea, and end up with a second one, by cleaning other people's house.

Jenna's story was that she wanted to start an online college counseling service for students but did not have the budgeted $2,600 to pay for the design of a proper service website, buy a dedicated computer, advertise it, and install a small office furnishing unit in her lower room.

Realizing her plight, she decided to offer a house cleaning service to the folks in her neighborhood for around $80 per home.

However, after working on the 14th house, and pocketing over a thousand dollars, Jenna began to receive referral calls from people outside of the neighborhood who learnt about her service through their workmates who had used it.

Overtime, Jenna was so overwhelmed with service requests that she made her required $2,600 within the first month, and still had over two dozen clients lined up.

This development led Jenna to consider establishing two small businesses instead.

And by the third month, her college counseling service website was running alongside her house cleaning service agency.

By the end of 2011, Jenna was running two businesses with 14 employees, and earning an average of $350,000 per year in profits, after deducting her taxes and all other expenses.

Using Jenna's experience, there is no doubt that our cash raising efforts can pay off dearly if we dedicate our efforts to our own cause.

Undertaking the house cleaning tasks for busy business professionals, families overwhelmed with work or families overwhelmed with kids, among other things; is one of the more older reliable methods for making additional cash.

You can advertise this service on your Church bulletin board, share flyers, or post an update on your Facebook page for free, so that friends, strangers and other interested parties can contact you as it relates to your services.

With this sort of task, you can bring in somewhere around $100 to 300 per day in extra earnings that can certainly aid your funding quest for your small business initiative.

And Finally ....

You can do what the Stovall's did

Many of the methods explained before hand, and the experience stories shared with a few of them, are testimonies to the many ways in which we can source funds and drive positive changes in our lives.

Many men and women dream of being able to stay home with their kids, but few families get to have both mom and dad stay home. Yet, that's exactly what has happened at the Stovall's house.

Jon and Stephanie Stovall both stay home with their kids and all because they finally found a work at home opportunity that really works.

Short on cash, Stephanie started looking for ways to make money from home almost 17 years ago.

After spending over $18,000 trying dozens of MLMs, Network Marketing businesses, gifting programs and anything else she could find, she was ready to quit.

But in September 1999, Stephanie's phone number ended up on a network marketing lead list.

She spoke with a guy who was consistently making $4,000 or more per week in a non-MLM business.

He told her about the incredible value of the Coastal travel package, and how she could make a minimum of $1,000 per sale.

The next day, Mrs. Stovall did some things that most people would see as rash: - she pawned the title to their only car at the local pawn shop, and then she dragged all her living room furniture out onto the front lawn and had a yard sale!

By the end of the first month, she made a total profit of $14,000, and raised just enough money to get her business started

Stephanie is now a top level Director selling travel packages worldwide and currently serves on a Board of Directors.

She is internationally recognized as an expert in the industry, has personally trained thousands of people to work from home successfully with Coastal, and expects to be doing this for years to come.

The Stovalls' really enjoy the freedom their business gives them. Stephanie only works 3-4 hours a day, yet earns enough to pay their bills and still travel the world with their children.

Working from home is a growing trend in America, and many, like the Stovalls', are finding new and more creative ways to make it possible.

.

Conclusion

Life is filled with thousands of home based business success stories, and a similar quantum of home based business failures too.

Interestingly, these successes and failures are often decided by the degree of funding that was injected into those home based business ideas, in addition to the overall dedication, direction, and management skills of the people behind those initiatives.

Almost every large company has a story to tell, and every large company started their history many years ago in the owner's garage or their living room, with either the funding or material loan backing of someone, somewhere.

From the borrowed $500 that made Bill Miller Bar-B-Que in San Antonio a multimillion dollar enterprise, to the $10,000 insurance check that made Master P the world's third richest rapper, there is always a success story to tell.

The foundations of everyone of those stories is always someone needing the money to make a seemingly simple home based business idea into a reality, and hopefully later, into corporate history.

It is in that sense that I have written this book, in the hope that you were able to utilize one or more of my 52 well thought out ideas to raise funds for your home based business.

In the end, I know you will have a success story to tell, and will certainly be another inspiration like the many others who had inspired you.

So, until you are ready to share your success story; -- Good luck on your home based business endeavors.

But before you go; - it will be great if you can garner some additional inspiration from the stories of a few other home based business owners, who was more than happy to share their testimonials with me, and by extension; with you.

Their success stories are based upon the application of funding recommendations that were mentioned earlier in this book, and ratified by their very actual experiences.

As such, I unhesitatingly invite you to take a peek at their own brief success stories that are imprinted in the final six pages of this book, which flows hereafter.

So, go ahead now, read their stories, ... and be inspired.

Our stories

"I am a single mom and do not receive any type of child support. So I don't typically have a lot of extra money after bills. I knew starting this business is something I wanted for me & my son. I wasn't sure how I would fund my business but after going through all my options I decided to do the loan. I took a loan against my 401K to fund my business". --- **Mandy Locklar**

"When I bought my starter package I was not even looking for a home base business. I was looking for a good deal on a vacation. When I found out I could get 7 night stays at nice resorts all over the U.S. for only $300.00. I bought the package using my credit card. I knew I could pay for my package with money I saved from one trip. I was so excited about the value of my package I wanted to find out what you needed to do to work the business". ---- **Mary Stephens**

"My husband worked many hours, and sometimes out of town. I wanted to be able to be home for our daughters when they were young. So, after coming across a home business, I knew It would be a way for me to work from home, and be able to have our family take many more vacations. We didn't have an extra money saved up, and bad credit! But I couldn't stop thinking about a way to come up with the investment. One day, while looking out my front window, dreaming of ways to get started. I happened to look down at my driveway, and saw my conversion van. Like a light bulb going off in my head, I realized right then that I could sell that conversion van, get started, and then with the money I make, I could buy something better down the road. And that is exactly what I did! I came in at the bottom and was able to step up to top position in a short time!" --- **Diana Fancher**

"I was miserable at my job in Corporate America and saved up enough money to be able to quit my six figure job after 16 years with the same company. I intended to live off my savings while finding that perfect job. Just a month later I found my home business and took money from my savings account and got started". --- **Kim Diaz**

"Prior to my home business, I felt extremely frustrated working a dead end job which was very stressful and I felt I wasn't getting paid enough for the effort. I was very tired of living paycheck to paycheck. I was not happy. I am a single mother with two boys and I felt very bad that I could not even afford things for them. I am so glad that I found my home business.

I got started the business using a credit card. Now, I am happy that I have something that I can count on making good income and be able to have time to travel and see places in the world with my boys and friends". **--- Jessica Man Wendelboe**

Prior to getting my current home business started and was a branch administrator in a leading insurance agency. Realizing quickly that I was making the other guy rich at my own person expense, I embark on an adventure in the home business arena. After trying many home businesses, I found that I was broke and heavily in debt. I found one more company but realize that it was thousands

of dollars to get started. Having no access to credit any more, I pawned all my DVD's and sold my favorite electronics. Within 7 months I generated over $100,000 working from my home. ---

Crystal Maguire

Prior to getting started in my current home business, I had already started and failed miserably in 13 other home based businesses. Then one day I was totally frustrated and about to give up my dream of being an entrepreneur until I saw an ad for another home based business. I needed real money to get started. So, I did something completely crazy.

I sold TV's, DVD collections, electronics. I still didn't have enough money. In desperation I convinced my husband to go to the bank to ask for a personal loan.

We were denied. However, I refused to give up. I swallowed my pride and I asked to borrow the rest of the funds from a relative. Luckily they said yes! I got to work in my new business and I made a handsome profit in my second week and paid off $25,000 in debt. ---

Heather Bahm

"I was a successful engineer in a very prestigious firm.

One day I was on a scaffolding, missed a step and suffered multiple injuries that forced me to lose my job.

I lost my home, wife, credit rating and purpose for a time. I was homeless barely making it on disability.

Not wanting to stay there, I pilfered my disability check and got started. Within my first year I generated over $140K in my home business and took me and my daughter China off the streets"

--- Avery Wadlington

"I am a high school teacher and I just finished my doctorate degree in October. I was working the after school program to attempt to earn the money to pay for the massive student loan.

I had never been so stressed out and time/energy depleted in my life. I literally had nothing left to offer my family at the end of the day. So I took out a loan for my top package and used my credit card for the business expenses". ---Leslie Baylis Chavez

---

Pawning the title to the family car and selling my living room furniture to get started in a home based business seemed really crazy. But I wanted to be a stay at home mom full time. I did not want to live in house that was in foreclosure anymore and living on public assistance was not a long term option for my family. My first year I made $94,000 and have not worked outside the home in over 14 years. --- **Stephanie Stovall**

---

www.ingramcontent.com/pod-product-compliance
Lightning Source LLC
Chambersburg PA
CBHW051315170526
45166CB00002B/553